THE ONLY WORLD

D1536780

To Virginia Salt[?]ner
with thanks and love,
Sept. 27. 1971

by Miller Williams

A CIRCLE OF STONE

RECITAL

19 POETAS DE HOY EN LOS ESTADOS UNIDOS

SOUTHERN WRITING IN THE SIXTIES: FICTION
(With John William Corrington)

SOUTHERN WRITING IN THE SIXTIES: POETRY
(With John William Corrington)

NICANOR PARRA: POEMS & ANTIPOEMS

SO LONG AT THE FAIR

CHILE: AN ANTHOLOGY OF NEW WRITING

THE ACHIEVEMENT OF JOHN CIARDI

THE ONLY WORLD THERE IS

THE ONLY WORLD
THERE IS

poems by
Miller Williams

E. P. DUTTON & CO., INC.   NEW YORK   1971

Published simultaneously in Canada by
Clarke, Irwin & Company Limited, Toronto and Vancouver

Library of Congress Catalog Card Number: 76-122786

SBN 0-525-17156-8 (Cloth)   SBN 0-525-04100-1 (Paper)

Grateful acknowledgment is made to the publications in which the
following poems first appeared:

The American Scholar: "The Assoc. Professor (Mad Scientist) to
  (His Love) . . ."
Brown Paper Bag: "Decade"; "A Letter to Cindy, Robert and Karen"
Concerning Poetry: "The House in the Vacant Lot"
The Denver Quarterly: "How a Sparrow Was Caught in My Trap . . .";
  "In Commemoration of the 20th Anniversary of the Ed Sullivan
  Show . . ."; "Love Poem"; "Today Is Wednesday"; "If Every Person
  There Is But One"; "How the Elephant Got His Hump"; "At the End
  of My Thirty-ninth Year"
The Falcon: "During a Language Lesson: for Karen"; "In Your Own
  Words Without Lying . . ."; "To Understand"; "Side Show"
Jeopardy: "Let Me Tell You"; "Vs the People"
Last Ditch: "Alcide Pavageau"
The Panamerican Review: "La Ultima Carta"
Partisan Review: "Revised Standard"
Pebble: "Poem: Untitled 1"; "Poem: Untitled 2 through 7"; "Then, If
  Ever"
Prairie Schooner: "Plain"
Prism International: "I Have Never"; "If You Can Answer This . . .";
  "My Father Who Is Seventy Five . . ."
Saturday Review: "Log"
Shenandoah: "N E T " under the title "E T V"
Virginia Quarterly Review: "It Is Not That It Came to Nothing
  Emiliano"

for CINDY

ROBERT

KAREN

Contents

THE ONLY WORLD THERE IS

Let Me Tell You

how to do it from the beginning.
First notice everything:
The stain on the wallpaper
of the vacant house,
the mothball smell of a
Greyhound toilet.
Miss nothing. Memorize it.
You cannot twist the fact you do not know.

Remember
The blonde girl you saw in the spade bar.
Put a scar on her breast.
Say she left home to get away from her father.
Invent whatever will support your line.
Leave out the rest.

Use metaphors: The mayor is a pig
is a metaphor
which is not to suggest
it is not a fact.
Which is irrelevant.
Nothing is less important
than a fact.

Be suspicious of any word you learned
and were proud of learning.
It will go bad.
It will fall off the page.

When your father lies
in the last light
and your mother cries for him,
listen to the sound of her crying.
When your father dies

take notes
somewhere inside.

If there is a heaven
he will forgive you
if the line you found was a good line.

It does not have to be worth the dying.

Today Is Wednesday

which is the day I have decided to understand.
I have tried since morning.
Now for the second time
my shadow is longer than I am
and still I can't understand.

I have asked everyone to help me.
I asked the busdriver to help me.
He said my name is John Foster Kelley
which is a name you will need.

I asked the waitress with mustard
on her mouth.
She said I have a surgical
scar on my belly.

I asked a policeman. I said
today is Wednesday.
He said go ask your mother.
I asked my mother.

I never saw you before in my life

son.

Tomorrow is Thursday.
Thursday I will understand.
If I can find the right bus
the right cafe
I will say
somebody help me.

Friday I will find myself
the one who can help me.

I will recognize it at once,
breasts of a big woman
face of a dog
the hinder parts held high
as a camel rises
in the unheated intergalactic spaces
under the gray blanket of my
most dry dreams

I will say *what about the whales*

and it will be done
Friday I will do it myself.

And I will tell everyone my understanding.
At first of course they will not hear
and when they do they will not allow me near
inhabited places.
I will grow old sending in scribbled notes
tied to the teats of cows and the tails of goats.

Side Show

Billboards sell me dirty miracles
the work of God gone bad.
Six girls their navels set with diadems
bumping their bottoms behind him
straddling invisible men not Methodists
the strawhatted preacher preaches
catches us running our tongues
around the girls.

eewolnks
eetolnks
eezalmos
chewmann
alive and breathing before your very
Look
(you think you got a skin problem
Lady
wait till you see the alligator woman)
fifty cents half a paper dollar.

The Alligator Woman
squats in her puddle
a dirty diaper slung
around her rear
an empty brassiere
pretending at the top
her legs crammed like crutches
into the hairy crotches of her arms.
She pulls at scabs
covering the best of her skin.
Something like milk leaks out.
She licks it away.

Hey over here
JoJo the Dogfaced Boy
found in the flats of Australia
naked and wild
by the famous Hiram Hinkleschitz
late of Harvard
raised by a band of marsupials
who took his mother
if you will forgive the expression
when she was a child.

JoJo barks
snaps at the legs
of a man and his giggling daughter
snarls how he could hurt
picks up his leg
against a post
makes the sound between his teeth
of dirt receiving water.

Fanny the Fat Lady
Fellows
Five hundred pounds a quarter
of a ton
the little bikini is bed sheets
put your misconceptions aside a second
try to imagine
you probably wonder how she got this way.
She was lithesome once as smoke
rising out of your house on a calm day.
She loved a man too much and when
she lost him
she consoled herself by feeding her flesh.
Her weight is a measure of her love.

The fat lady moves her face to a laugh and squeaks,
her glistening dugs move barely and slip back,

settle slowly, sleep soft and heavy
as slugs.
She crams a candy bar between her cheeks.

See the Siamese Twins the Inseparable Sisters:
See the one that has the frowning face.
Today is Thursday. Thursday is the day
for her to stumble backwards
to see the world jerk away.
Both of the ladies are virgins
I need not say
and they will be virgins
sleeping on their sides
the happy one careful
the sad one careful to scratch
no itch not her own by definition.

I don't like to mention
which is why I whisper
the next
well
person
out of respect for
consider
what must be the
lord
embarrassment
please do not stare
out of common respect
who has to earn a living
revealing those parts
I cannot mention for lord the innocent ears.

Something inside you've never dreamed of.

Friday morning
walking to work

I listen to each tap tell me
though girls are dancing everywhere I go
though the clouds hang loose from pole to pole
I walk on two legs in a world of sidewalks
and am real
and have a pedestrian and unprofitable soul.

La Ultima Carta: A Young Venezuelan Wife Writes to Her Husband in the Mountains

I make a Y
brittle as dry wood.
The sputtering pen splits open
unwrites words I could not have mailed.

Saturday I sat by the lake
pretended to read letters
that have not come.
They are too brief and tell me you are well.
I am not sure I believe them.

Under my hand, Husband
brooms break
corn grinds to sand.

You have no faith in spirits
would claim the water
dripping from a tap at night
means nothing
that a wind coming down to the coast
out of those hills is neither alive nor dead
but I listen for signs

and forgive me this:
when the wind
brushes against the curtain
touches my sheet
I tense to feel the fingers of a ghost.

I look through my eyes in the morning mirror
afraid I will conjure you
trying to conjure you there

but all I see are the days spinning back
with the strange quiet violence of dreams.

Sra. Cortinez whose son was a good soldier
is also alone and knows she is going
to be alone. I envy her knowing
for certain. Forgive me.

I sit up late
after unweaving myself
and write you letters
and everytime the thought comes
that you may go and I not
know about it

that I may write a month
after your death
to tell you things
as one talks meaningfully with gestures
to a friend who half a block back
has stopped at some store,
that I will hold your picture
focus on your mouth
to remember you more
while in some obscene place
a snake is crawling through your face.

I tell you my unfaithfulness
my unforgivable sin
that I am no longer sure my letters
keep you alive

but I will keep on writing
until we win
what we are fighting for
whoever we are.

It Is Not That It Came to Nothing
Emiliano

It is not that it came to nothing
Emiliano.
All things do.
It is that it came
in a slow land
so quickly true.

There is a rope
a campesino will take a tourist to see
for two pesos
that has not even rotted from the tree.

It is not that he died for nothing
Emiliano.
So all men die.
It is that he went
in a slow land
so suddenly by.

There is a temple
a precarious cone of rocks some men built here
before Christ
to please the seasons and divide the year.

It is not that your dreams died.
Dreams do.
All dreams are grass.
It is how soon
Emiliano
it came to pass.

Log

It is Sunday.

There are two wars.

In four days
not counting border outbreaks
and rebellious acts

seventy thousand lay down dead
who were not ill or old
and did not fall off ladders.

Two blocks from where I am
words on a laundromat
appear to say

WHITE ONLY

The words are in code: they say

A DECREE WENT OUT

they say

I OWN A LAUNDROMAT AND I AM MAD

they say

KILL

It is the sign of his madness
he can write in codes
he does not know.

Plain

Out of Mobile I saw a 60 Ford
fingers wrapped like pieces of rope
around the steering wheel
foxtail flapping the head of the hood
of the first thing ever
he has called his own.

Between two Bardahls
above the STP
the flag flies backwards
Go To Church This Sunday
Support Your Local Police
Post 83
They say the same thing
They say
I am not alone.

July 20, 1969

I

The Los Angeles Times
The Russellville, Arkansas Courier-Democrat
The movie marquee in Pottsville, Minnesota
for instance
say Go

It is not the word
because there is no word
for what we think
are almost sure
we feel

We sit in our living rooms and see the moon tracked
by the boots of men

We knew the myth
for being something other than fact
was true

When fact and truth fall together
we say something is real
as for instance
an orange

Sermons in the city say yes
in the country no

Two o'clock in the morning
clear channel
preachers
sending grace and glory to watchmen
huddled over heaters
cooks in truckstops

old women
living alone

cry Babel
      Babel

nor stone be left on stone

Looking good. Looking good.

The Kingdom is at hand

gimme
narseena
moompie
please

II

We stand in the crowds
in the street
something like prayer
and watch the heaviest moon
come out of the clouds

I want to take off my clothes
she says
and think about them

they will need me here
on the face of the earth

She slides to a tree
and climbs it
like a lizard
climbing out of her clothes

She is up there somewhere

If she is still human
If it is still today in the top of the tree
she will come down

What preacher
in what poor pulpit
will look up his lines
in Fifty-Two Soul-Saving Sermons
this good coming Sunday

So What some say So What

Even a man who is pure in heart
and says his prayers at night
may become a werewolf
when the wolfbane blooms
and the autumn moon is bright

III

According to Korea's Calendar of the Moon
this is four thousand six hundred sixty seven

Perigee to Perigee
is known as the anomalistic month

According to Korea's Calendar of the Moon
this is the Year of the Chicken
in which it is written
Admiral Peary reached the North Pole
Hitler came to power
Hitler Roosevelt Mussolini Quisling
Hiroshima and Nagasaki died
Faubus was famous
Sputnik I

little moon of mystery and a people's pride
moon of no gods
beeped its jealous way around the world
Three men flew to the moon and made a landing
A girl was born in Caruthersville, Missouri

Which may or may not be true

I report as it was reported to me
which is all an annalist can do
not understanding

IV

Earth
the coast of Africa
becoming horizon
falling away
blue planet
smooth as a catseye

under the marbling clouds
cows are munching toward barns and the new night
are moving out to pasture
in the first light of day

Husbands and wives
argue themselves to bed
wait for the toast
stare at the table
to think what it was they said
of something to say

Soldiers in a line
lean forward
like firemen
pulling a hose

move through writhing water
over deserts

the earth lifts up to meet the feet
where the line goes

Altitude 700. Drifting right.

I mean if God would of meant us to be there

Contact light. OK. Engine stop.

In Caruthersville, Missouri
a girl turned twelve
bleeds on the bed in her sleep

This day
This night This
moon's orbit
Sunday
a priest gets married
a bus goes off the road

in Santiago, Chile
Nicanor Parra
watches the low moon
sink lower
feels her behind him
turns and understands
and closes the door

By this full light
two thousand one hundred years
before we saw it
Hannibal betrayed
killed himself in Bithynia

The earth is clean from here
as in the beginning

no paperclips no bottles
no battlefields

Dave
what are you doing

no borders

nothing

one planet
perfect edges
blurred by the sun
spinning motionless through space
the first blue syllable of the unspoken word

Engine stop.
We copy you down Eagle.

Eagle

That word was coming to be
when all words were young
before the last ice left to leave to man
the Pyrenees and the Mediterranean Sea

What sound was made to say moon
in that old tongue

V

Māno / menë
Goddess of the Moon

Māno / Mōn / Mēn
Moon God of Asia

Sin
Sumerian
Moon God
Lord of All Wisdom
Lover of the Goddess Níngal
Creator of Gods

dream themselves again back into being
dream us to dream them

Sin Shamash and Ishtar
stir
come conscious

under the Palatine Hills

remember how
where   what it was
to be

feel the inpouring power
of earthly wills
saying

Sin Shamash Ishtar

saying One
saying Three

We copy you down.
Tranquillity Base here.
The Eagle has landed.

The God who is God sits down

feels a sleep come on him
His woman sits down beside him
and speaks of their son

and Sin remembers Níngal
in the temple at Ur

In Commemoration of
the 20th Anniversary of the Ed Sullivan Show
and Every Anniversary Following

Let's hear it for the Lord's Prayer

dogs dressed for dinner
dance inhumanly
but singers sing
acrobats tumble and Frank Meriwell
stands in the audience and waves.

There is gladness and ease across the land.

Absolutely, Mr. Gallagher? Positively, Mr. Sheen.

I sing you praise nobody will believe
catatonic talker for a score
of W-2s and Easters
best listener in the world
may you listen for more.
I send you praise nobody will believe
who never wrote for Dylan Thomas
or Roethke
who never wrote a public line to grieve
for the President of the United States and Style
for Medgar Evers whose killer most nearly was mine
for Martin Luther King despised
of madmen
for Flannery O'Connor
who let my children
chase her flowering peacocks
a little while
for Robert Kennedy who was never surprised.
For all of them nothing

nothing about the war
who would have gladly
who began and began

The form can never be smaller than what it holds.
That is a fact, Flannery. Forgive the fact.

RARE FISH FOUND IN INDIAN OCEAN

Port Elizabeth, South
Africa (AP)—Rhodes
University Scientist
L.L.B. Smith, using
a color photograph,
identified a white-
blotched, velvety black
fish found in the Indian
Ocean as one of the rarest
in the world.
Back in an aquarium
the fish died and was
eaten by crabs.

Beginning and beginning
who could write a poem about that?
The form has got to be harder than what it holds.
That is a fact, Flannery. Forgive the fact.

So saying I sing Ed Sullivan whose 20 rounds
have held the wars and The War and the children spilled
The walls of Newark darker dawn by dawn
The president killed, Evers fixed and forgotten.
Flannery gone.

Here in New Orleans only uneasily warm
sitting out only a summer thunder shower
I write for the fish I scratch in the hard dirt

the sullen stand-in
always the means to an end
and praise him to cry for all the dead children
I have cared for in fact and the act only

in bumper stickers and sit-ins and checks
and on my daughter's bedroom door, a flower.

Next week on our stage
direct from the land
where the Mustang and buffalo roam
Malcolm X
the poets Dylan Thomas and Medgar Evers
O'Connor the Catholic
the Kennedys and King
Roosevelt Jackson and all the dead children
one Homer Tuttle who sits quietly at home
and is startled to hear his name and does not understand.

Then, If Ever

being a plan in breakable code
for the overthrow of governments
and holy institutions

I

When every mouth is fed
and every head has eyes and ears
and a good girl fears her father's bed
never

II

When the last faithful father
has left the son to his mother
and gone to the bed
of his most patient lover

When they are married
by broomstick
and stay home

and all the mad drivers
the drunken ticket takers
of mass transit
have run into bridge abutments
with empty buses

are wrapped in black rags
and carried away

III

When all the marching men are naked

and can't find their clothes

anywhere in the world ever

How a Sparrow Was Caught in My Trap
When I Was Ten
and Covered with Lice
So I Killed It

And I recall how far I fell toward fact
to something like truth when those inlooking eyes
went to peace in the godhood of my hand

and left in me this dark and slow surprise
that gnaws like a faithful cancer at the host.
On the silent television stuck in my skull

the blind faces of children are bright as candles
the rump of a rooster gets himself up to crow
I see the soldiers crawling world without end.

The darkness in our hearts is not what we think.
We ask how this could happen. We pretend.
The darkness in our hearts is that we know.

Voice of America

Do not imagine his father lying
between his mother and falling to sleep
beside her while she wonders how
she knows, knowing she will keep

the secret for a weaker proof.
Do not imagine the million seed
moving by some myotic hunger
from dark to dark, from need to need.

Do not imagine one by luck
or fate finds the target to win
and like a bullet hitting a head
in slow motion crashes in.

Do not imagine the man starts
and terminates in the same act,
will be before the bullet stops
the zero absolute unfact

his mother remembered in reverse.
Do not imagine his father sent
the million missiles against the egg
with more joy and less intent.

Do not imagine the cells splitting.
Do not imagine the hollow ball
he was awhile, a senseless worm,
no heart, head, nothing at all,

as when his father a following day
the following month would ask "What is it?"
"It's nothing. It's honestly nothing at all."
Do not imagine the exquisite

danger when the cell divides
when a chromosome splits apart
half shifting here, half there,
to shape the kidney and the heart.

Do not imagine the enormous eyes.
Do not imagine the chin sits
soft against the uncovered heart.
Do not imagine the gill slits,

the hands unfinished, the tail shrinking.
Do not imagine the time at hand
or what it means. Raise the gun.
Hold it gently as you were trained

to hold it. Let the bullet swim
slowly into his opening head
fast as sperm   the way the films
in school can show a flower spread.

Revised Standard: The New Testament

This we have lost

free will
the *a priori*

We cannot say for an hour
the sun stood still
Sing Glory

Yet our fathers are kept alive
in us all

By insulated entrails
Belshazzar computes

We are reluctant to die

Men keep count for kings and
good causes

Ezekiel shoots the sky

So what if only nuns and Baptists
believe in miraculous birth

we have not lost our fathers

They are with us always in love
to the ends of the earth

Vs the People

Do you swear?

To What?

To tell the truth.

I will make distinctions
where they matter.

What is your name?

An old condition
I have not overcome.

Where were you on the night of the twenty-third?

I was committing crimes against the State.

How do you plead?

How should I know?

Think about your dog when you were seven.

And what else?

Think of the first girl you got your hands on.

And what else?

Think of the Hindenburg bursting into bloom.

And what else?

Think about two o'clock in the morning.

If that is so
yes, I confess:
I have spoken to strangers

It is my duty to warn you.

I have spread the word.
I told the preacher
the truth
I told the judge
I told the teacher telling of Abraham Lincoln
his children would know he was lying
and would eat his ears.

Who took the bomb into the power plant?

I did not vote for the president or my
mother.

Who blew up the bridge?

Jelly can be made also from apples.
The president
is in many ways my mother.

I am your mother.
What is your name?

It is still the same:
8-99-4-914.

I do not want to play
this game
anymore.

How the Elephant Got His Hump

for John Christman

Consider a fact: an olive
(unlike cherries and boysen
berries and beans) begins
as a most potent poison.

An olive grower of course
and biochemist know what'll
make it the bitter and dun
hors d'oeuvre we buy in a bottle.

The olive is soaked in lye
for twenty days and turned
on every one of the twenty
to keep it from being burned

then soaked in the juice of pickles
and turned every day
which renders the amine soluble
enough to be leached away

the amine being the problem
which amine being bound
to a protein makes an olive
which falls upon the ground

so deadly quick a poison
which is why the lye
has first to break the bond
which of course is why

no man of the Middle East
or beast has ever been seen

or seen again if he was
eating an olive green.

The question before the house:
Since the receipt is now
4,000 years old at least
who found it out, and how?

Well, I have a fancy.
Imagine the high priest
Lord Executioner
of all the Middle East

preparing to put to death
a breaker of taboos
who diddled the temple virgins
and never paid his dues

in the shabby lodge he lived in
and pissed in the sacred pool
slept at sacrifices
and toyed with his tool

until he roused the anger
of elders and what was worse
perverse admiration
until a public curse

was said upon his head.
The High Priest swore to make
a more than common end
and set about to take

the fruit which was by custom
exquisite execution,
to cook it first in a caustic,
second an acid, solution.

When he contemplated
the agony in his hand
he could only smile
that he could understand

how he had come to be
the number one High Priest
Lord Executioner
of all the Middle East.

To make more perfect perfection
and imperfect people the humbler
he poured the *coup de grace*
two poisons in a tumbler

juice of the fruit and grain
said to drive men mad
and mixed them 5 to 1
by chance and knew he had

when he dropped in the olive
such agony in the cup
that he could scarcely speak
to summon the buglers up

to the top of the highest hill
where desert turns to sky
to summon the people in
to watch the heretic die.

The heretic being of gentle
birth albeit a fool
was set to lose his life
but would not lose his cool.

He took the drink as told to
and killed it in a swallow

and asked his host politely
if there was more to follow.

He nibbled the olive even
to take fate's roughest ration
and spat the pit at the people
and posed in a manly fashion

and was not less surprised
to find he would not die
than those prostrate about him
who called him Highest of High.

As King he showed his people
his powers were still alive
by drinking a draft of poison
each afternoon at five

for all the years of his reign
which were forty and four
and said that it was good
and often called for more

prepared of course by him
who once was Lord High Priest
who now was Royal Mixer
to the King of the Middle East.

The House in the Vacant Lot

Cutting across a vacant lot
I felt concrete under my feet
and found myself at the front door
of a house that was not there anymore.

I traced the walls by where the grass
was thin and came again to the spot
where the entrance hall had been.
I let myself as it seemed to me in

and wandered through the disappeared
and long-forgotten rooms. Some glass
and a broken brick were all that was left
of the rooms where people had kissed and slept

once alone and together once.
I thought of this and then a weird
or common thought took hold of my head:
Why do I think of the past as dead?

Am I a person present and real
walking through a house that by chance
was and is not or am I he
who am not but who will be

who steps through real and present brick?
Or am I here and the house here still?
Is some woman's heartbeat quicker
when she sees the candle flicker

in a closed room? Are we together?
Does such commingling twist and crack
windows I walk through? Does a cold fear
come? Do they wonder if I walk here?

When a glass tumbles does the mother
cross herself? Does the priest
come to say that I am Christ
or to exorcize the poltergeist?

If Every Person There Is But One

If every person there is but one
should disappear
and then all cats
birds grass
seahorses trees
all rocks and water and toys
and all planets the same
and the suns go out and the ashes
blow away in the winds
and the winds go
and the man explodes in bright silence
to atoms
and all the atoms dissolve to darkness
but one
which being the center
of weight and all dimension
can never
no matter how fast
move away
from the middle

that moving is not moving
We have been tricked

The atom you may say
is also nothing
and so put aside the problem
but let us say
with a fump and flash of light
and a splash of water
everything is back
and I walk across the street

by what argument do I not
when I get there
stand in dead center
still

Think of whatever moves
as God / or if nothing moves

think how still we stand

Decade

We know an awful lot of mathematics.
There are whole towns of houses with no attics.

If You Can Answer
This There Are No
More Questions

How do you know
when you choose
(you say)
to
you could have
not to?

This is a warning

Ergo

Under a streetlamp
to his teachers applause
long as can be allowed by dreams laws
he opens his pants
and pees
on a hill of ants.

His pencil streams a message:

I am a cause.

To Understand

what it means to cough
fall sick, die, rigor, soften and rot

and be everywhere absent
being pulled apart

is neither easy nor useful
is probably good

is this:

to imagine a language
that is not

as Demosthenes
might have heard

in the sea

the impossible verbs
of English

and understood.

NET

Too tired to sleep I switch a picture on
turn down the sound to let attention drain.
A dark forest. Dogs. A man is running.
It is starting to rain.

The man comes to a house. He breaks a window.
A girl getting out of the shower admiring herself
looks to see if the cat has knocked something
from the kitchen shelf.

She sees the man. She wraps her towel about her.
In the woods loosed from their leashes the dogs
are running in circles scratching at empty trees
sniffing at logs.

The woman is breathing behind a chair in the kitchen.
The man is leaning against the kitchen door.
Her mouth moves. He hits her across the face.
She falls to the floor.

He tears the towel away. Her eyes go wild.
She is naked. He looks. He lets her curl
into a corner. He kneels down. His hands
discover the girl.

He takes her to her bed and puts her in it.
Looks at her face as if he has not seen her
until now. Takes off his clothes and puts
himself between her.

She smiles. He smiles. She bends her knees and locks him.
They are moving together. I turn up the sound.
They stop. They turn their heads. They see me.
A single hound

is crouping close. Face frozen in rage or fear
she rolls out of bed. Runs with nothing around her
into the rain, into the leaping dogs
the theological thunder.

He sits on the bed, his back a slow curve.
The door opens. A man with a long gun.
Jesus. Forgive me. I do not know
what I have done.

The Assoc. Professor (Mad Scientist) to (His Love) His Student in Physics 100 Lab

What you have to know
$F=MA$
is what you have to know

a slow truck can break you
quick
as a fast brick

two that want love a little will lay
more likely than one
wanting love a lot

if God is anything more than simply not
he has only barely to be
so capital is the G

and you
if you turn your head
can
as a matter of course
dismiss my class

if you turned your body and
smiled
immorally illegally
I wonder
what could I do
with such a sudden force
with such a mass

I Have Never

been to a bull fight.
Sunday I saw one when the Cards were called
and nothing worth watching was happening
anywhere.

> Trumpets
> The beast
> The truth broke out like sap
> in the colored cup
> in the first of all the fights
> he was born for
>
> The monster fell in flowers
> A hard shiver
> shook out the last of his lights

Well yes, Mother.

It was black & white.

There weren't any flowers at all.

It was on the radio.

I lie a lot.

Which is what it's all about
which is not to say
I tell you anything but what is true
about the bull fight
which was in Monterrey:
the horns were a lobster's claws
the balls were blue
the sword was love in the matador's right hand.

Do you understand?

Do you understand?

Poem: untitled 1

Can you tell me

YOU ARE GO FOR
TLI

which is the way

ROGER

to Ireland

Poem: untitled 2 through 7

And if there are minds
on Mars
if the first man finds
movie stars
and oyster bars
and pot
and no word for God
then what

and if there are minds
on Venus
if the first man finds
a genus
all penis
and squat
and no word for love
then what

and if there are minds
so far
that no man finds
their star
dream sailors there
that one
sights through his sails
our sun

Alcide Pavageau

Slow Drag Dead

hallelulia

four black Cadillac

high black hearse

and all

the people come

to hear the trom

bone bawl

look at Slow

Drag picture on

the Wall

He call again

Sweet Emma come

Big Jim come when He call

then honkie play

and honkie plunk

in Preservation

Hall

In Your Own Words Without Lying
Tell Something of Your Background
with Particular Attention
to Anything Relating to the Position
for Which You Are Applying:　　Press Down

Pressing down I remember
the night my father
and mother will have forgotten:
she filled the lamps in the kitchen
he slung the washing water on the ground
chickens scattered squawking;
the sound of the pump primed
the cold zinc of the dipper
water down the chin
a mumbled word
and the long yawn at last
that leaves the body hollow as a gourd
when the vegetable skin
goes brown and hard
under the thick green vines
in the dry yard
And they went to bed
the night I came together
and began.

I may have been describing the night
my grandfather
emptied himself of my father
and my never uncles.
There was no way to tell the difference
in those nights.

I think that was the first important thing.

I was covered when I was five
like Job with boils
they shaved my head
peeled the cloth away from the bed
in the morning.
I slept
propped on hands and knees
my mother kept me clean
my forehead against the floor
the doctor stayed
while my father who was a
preacher prayed.
The neighbors came to call
said What have you done
that God has put this affliction on your son.

When I was eleven I went to sleep
with a gothic radio underneath the quilt
the glowing grin of the dial
bright as the guilt I manufactured there.

Saturday night the Grand Old Hayride
There's A Great Speckled Bird
Flying Somewhere
But I Didn't Hear Nobody Pray.

Sunday nights I listened to the prophets,
how faith washes sins and Catholics away:

This is Brother Bob's Good Old Gospel Hour
Our time is almost
send your dimes and dollars
The Bible Man
B-I-B-L-E
We depend
to help us carry on
to the first two thousand

a plastic table cloth
that glows
in the dark
with the face of Jesus

Imagine what your friends and neighbors will say

while the choir sings one more time
in the background softly

and tenderly Jesus is calling
O Sinner Come Home.

Monday Miss Gardner began the fifth grade
took up the marbles
let Big Butt Butler erase the board
never me
sent sealed messages to other rooms
by Salina Mae who was already starting
to have tits Walter said were got
from doing it.

O. D. showed what he had behind the gin
always after Salina Mae was gone
and Mary Sue let us look if we begged her.

Walter drowned.
O. D. is a doctor. Mary Sue married
a preacher and has children.
Salina Mae I will tell you about.

One Saturday Afternoon we made believe

That is all I can tell

On my grandfather's farm
there was a river we swam in
there was an old bell to call us back

My Father Who Is Seventy Five
Will Not Thank God for His Years

> ". . . children ardent for some desperate
> glory. . . ."   Wilfred Owen

He imagines how a child not his
crawls across the floor
and calls his name
bubbles into flame and disappears

He imagines the smell in his kitchen
of smoldering hair
imagines that burning fingers
curl like snakes

He sleeps to see me standing in the door
blazing

He wakes to find me not there
and alive
is embarrassed to be glad

I know that he is

But come to seventy five my father
will not thank God for anything that is his

During a Language Lesson: for Karen

What is it that a genius knows?
Karen there are mostly those
who talk parabolas I suppose
but others if only a very few
say wissenschaft

not as men of science do.
What genius are you pointing to?
The one that in a season drew
the bright curving of your clothes
by wiccecraeft?

At the End of My Thirty-ninth Year

I

I came
being no country's king
without a bugle or flag or drum
or angels to sing
or anything
not even silver in my eyes
the eighth day of the fourth month
when the only thing to fear was fear
though my father would not know that
for another year.

There was no sign
for my aunts to see
in the cow's milk or the dog's hair
that I should be blest
and loved or curst
so they laid me down and left me there
equally out of hope and despair
to nothing but luck and the New Deal
and the mercy of God and my mother's breast.

The cards were all cornered.
Fear was a radio that eats the earth.

But luck and mercy have lasted.

My brothers came home.

She was not pregnant.

I am almost forty.

II

All of which is a way of saying look.

III

A friend has come by after twenty years.
I am a little sadder than before he came.
The nervous socialist no longer moves
across my memory when I think the name.

He has come into my house and killed himself.
He is here. He is not. It has been too long.
He sits with his wife as we trade remembering
and looks at me as if I remember wrong.

IV

When mercy grows tired of mercy or luck fails
let me remember in all hospitals jails
let me remember rightly your hands and feet
the places where your nakedness and mine meet

that we are together here a better time
than luck even alone or mercy can bear
which is to say I have not understood
the meaning of this or the meaning of anything much

of the sign in the cow's milk that was not there
to tell of anything or the dog's hair
except as there are no signs. Except as we breathe.
Except as we barely touch. And leave off breathing.

A Letter to Cindy, Robert & Karen
Being various precepts and admonitions toward a good life
and perhaps long

Against lessons learnt
against plans for war
actuarial tables
the good sense of remembering nothing

I set this down:

there is a capsule I will bury
to be found
when it is old enough to be important.
This as you know now was in it.

I have only eleven things to tell you.

Cindy first, a reminder. Write it down.
In the beginning was the word
and the word was withdrawn.
Which brings me to your question

about the aluminum temple in New York:
the answer is no.

Robert:
Learn to kick.
If you aren't that mad you will lose anyway.
Go home.

Most girls had rather be kissed
inside the elbow
but the tip of the tongue on the corner of her mouth
will do it.
You have known this for a long time.

Karen: Be careful of trucks coming toward you
of mad men with knives
of policemen. They are necessary
to full employment and a sane nation.
Do not trust them.

When you begin to drive
as you have done
what you must remember is this
about the young man
who at the corner of Canal and Magazine
lets you in line:
he has been a part of your life a moment.
You will never see him again.
When he has gone to bed
twenty thousand times
with the same woman
lost ten thousand hands
of poker and his teeth
you will not be a wrinkle
in his brain
who held him long enough
from some sudden intersection
once.
Think of this when you learn to drive.

And for the three of you these three things:

Remember your names and the names of your
grandfathers.
Remember the hills of earth.

There is a story you will have to read. Read it.

I have gone past eleven.

We love you. I tell you this directly and
without embarrassment.
Try not to think about it too much.

Love Poem

Six o'clock and
the sun rises across the river.
The traffic cop wakes up and
crawls over his wife.
The naked professor will sleep another hour.
The dentist wakes up and reaches for a smoke.
The doctor reaches for the phone
and prescribes
his voice full of rust.
The shoeclerk wakes to his clock
touches himself
and lies listening to his woman in the shower.

It is midnight now in Samoa.

Nine o'clock and
the school bell rings.
Miss Gardner taps her ruler on the desk.
She calls the roll.
Oscar Carpenter is absent.
He does not like the sound of the ruler.

It is midnight now in Osaka.

Eleven o'clock:
The salesman makes his way past dogs and wheels
his knuckles already sore
hoping for bells
On Maple Street the policeman's wife
shuts her kimono slowly and shuts the door.
On Willow Street the professor's wife
tells him about her cousin in Mineral Wells
who was also a salesman but never amounted to much.

On Juniper Street the dentist's wife
is drunk and lets him have her on the floor
says she will get a divorce
says she will see him again of course if she can.

It is midnight now in Djakarta.

Five o'clock and
the men are coming home.
The traffic cop comes home
his ears in his pockets.
The doctor comes home
the sun slipping down his forehead.
The shoeclerk comes
The uncertain knees
still fitting the sockets of his eyes.

It is midnight now in Berlin.

Six o'clock:
The streetlights come on.

It is midnight now in Bordeaux.

Ten o'clock:
In Mercy Hospital a man is dying.
His brain
squeezes all his thoughts to one thought
squeezes that to nothing
and lets go.

It is midnight now in La Paz.

Eleven o'clock:
The children are gone to bed and we are here
sitting across the room from one another
accustomed to this house

that is not ours to keep
to this world that is not ours
and to each other.

Sands run through the children in their sleep.

About the Author

MILLER WILLIAMS teaches in the creative writing program at the University of Arkansas. He is noted as an editor, anthologist, and translator, most recently in *Chile: An Anthology of New Writing*. His critical works include *John Crowe Ransom, His Poems* and *The Achievement of John Ciardi*.

He lives with his wife and three children in Fayetteville, Arkansas.